MARKIE LUFIES

DEEPER CONNECTION

Contents

INTRODUCTION

How might this benefit me? Figure out how to associate with others in a split second.

We as a whole know the inclination: we meet somebody for the absolute first time at a party, or maybe in line at the mailing station and a split second become quick companions.

We click.

For what reason does this occur? In Snap, siblings Ori and Rom Brafman research the powers behind this peculiarity and recommend substantial ways that we can achieve momentary associations, or what the creators call speedy set closeness.

The accompanying flickers give you many key bits of knowledge about the extraordinary elements of speedy set closeness. For instance, you'll figure out why we experience "click minutes" as significant and why such significant associations matter extraordinarily to our prosperity (answer: discouragement is exceptionally uncommon in affectionate networks).

You'll realize the reason why meeting somebody interestingly can make you high and how those absolute first minutes can loan a supernatural quality to the remainder of a relationship.

You'll figure out why a prisoner moderator would enlighten a prisoner taker concerning the day his mom kicked the bucket.

Furthermore, you'll try and find the reason why sharing a residence could spike a reliably terrible b-ball group onto an extraordinary series of wins.

connecting is the point at which you out of nowhere feel an exceptionally pleasurable, nearly "supernatural" association.

Think about this recognizable scene:

Two outsiders end up gathering someplace - maybe it's on a train, during a long excursion. One of them sees the other is perusing a book by their number one essayist and can't avoid referencing it. In a split second, the pair are attracted to one another and as they begin to visit about various things, every one of them starts to feel as though they've known the other individual for as long as they can remember.

This is connecting and it's quite possibly the most agreeable thing you can insight.

Why?

One fundamental explanation is that we experience connecting as a sort of happiness.

In one examination, neuroscientists filtered the cerebrums of individuals who'd clicked in an especially heartfelt manner: they'd experienced passionate feelings. The outputs showed that those regions of the cerebrum for the most part connected with pleasurable encounters were extraordinarily dynamic. The degree of movement that the researchers noticed ordinarily demonstrates a condition of happiness - a degree of delight regularly set off by drugs like cocaine.

Another explanation is that we will generally consider connecting as significant. Without a doubt, we frequently even experience it as nearly "otherworldly."

At the point when one clinician requested a different gathering of individuals to review a practically supernatural encounter, out of the relative multitude of occasions of their altogether different lives a great many people named unequivocally those minutes when they'd encountered a moment association with somebody.

One lady, for example, portrayed how she and an outsider had locked eyes and were struck by a prompt feeling of shared closeness. In no time, they'd turn into a couple.

Moreover, practically every one of the members utilized similar characteristics to portray those minutes; they called them invigorating, exciting, extraordinary, or euphoric. In any event, when a similar inquiry was presented to a unique gathering, they utilized precisely the same descriptive words.

So connecting can make us ridiculously cheerful and might make us accept that in those minutes when our lives converge with those of others, we are encountering something strange.

connecting makes connections extraordinary.

What's something significant that prompts a cheerful marriage? Is it that the two individuals like each other in an extraordinary arrangement? Or on the other hand, is it that they share a lot of interests?

Or on the other hand, maybe there's such an incredible concept as all-consuming, instant adoration.

At the point when clinicians researched this very subject, they found an astonishing relationship: those wedded couples who'd encountered a prompt and extraordinary association when they initially met had a more enthusiastic marriage.

In the review, specialists contrasted couples and different heartfelt narratives. In the first place, there were those couples who were companions before starting a heartfelt connection. Second, some had to deal with a conventional romance period. In conclusion, there were those couples who'd fallen frantically enamored the second they met.

What they found was that even following 25 years of marriage, a couple that had encountered head-over-heels love kept on contrasting from one another recognizably, though in the initial two gatherings the life partners were significantly more like one another.

Be that as it may, the couples whose relationship started with an enthusiastic first experience likewise kept on showing the most significant levels of enthusiasm, even after over twenty years.

Maybe one justification behind this is that, with regards to a "supernatural" first experience, a whole relationship will show up as something uniquely great.

Think about Nadja and Paul, for instance. These two initially met working and from the very beginning, both detected an extraordinary quality to their gathering and communication. To such an extent, that after only three days Paul requested that Nadja wed him.

after 15 years, even though their relationship was not without its difficulties, the flash that had at first drawn them to one another still loans that otherworldly quality to their relationship and keeps them endeavoring to make the relationship work.

As these models show, connecting can loan an extraordinary quality to the connections that it starts. Without a doubt, the very enthusiasm that made you high when you initially met will keep on starting your shared association, whether it's companionship or a heartfelt connection.

We perform better in the organization of individuals we click with.

Shockingly, the progress of a string group of four relies predominantly upon one sole component - that the performers click with one another. Be that as it may, how could connecting have such a significant impact on the effective communication of prepared experts?

One explanation is that a gathering who snaps imparts all the more successfully, which, thusly, can bring about expanded capability.

Think about those individuals in a cozy relationship. They seem to comprehend each other with practically no work. For example, they need to utilize fewer words to impart successfully and to get their point across - and that implies fewer mistaken assumptions.

For a string group of four, the fundamental advantage of connecting in this way is that the players will want to perceive melodic signals absent a lot of exertion by any stretch of the imagination.

Another advantage is that the people who snap can examine troublesome issues in a positive, productive way. For instance, a string group of four must frequently examine how they are to decipher a piece of music. On the off chance that the gathering clicks, any contentions that emerge in such a conversation aren't for the most part about declaring one's situation in the gathering at the same time, but rather, the music.

Interestingly, less all-around adjusted groups of four don't determine clashes over melodic understanding. All things being equal, everybody adheres to his adaptation. The outcome? A significantly less durable presentation.

A further advantage of a connecting group is that it's significantly more liable to continue through troublesome times and one justification behind this is that its individuals are essentially more strong than one another. For instance, the individuals from a very much adjusted string group of four will generally pull for their kindred entertainers and care about their prosperity.

At long last, a group that snaps is likewise more imaginative and ready to make unpredictable, in any event, trying choices. In one examination, MBA understudies in bunches that clicked went up against bunches that didn't. Each gathering was told to perform undertakings that were inconsequential to their field of study and new to them. The outcome? The gatherings that clicked outflanked different gatherings by greatness of 20 to 70 percent.

On the off chance that you make yourself defenseless against others, you're bound to click with them.

How could a prisoner moderator enlighten a threatening detainer concerning the day his mom kicked the bucket? It seems like a plot point from a film, however it worked out.

Besides, it was precisely this disclosure that undeniably a defining moment in the discussion.

Why?

Assuming you intentionally make yourself weak by uncovering your feelings, shortcomings, and fears, you sign to others that you trust them. Thusly, those individuals will be bound to trust you and instinctually respond by making themselves defenseless as well.

The receptiveness that this elevates can prompt a personal association being laid out. At the point when you open up to somebody, they'll for the most part decipher this as an encouragement to strengthen the relationship. Assuming they open up as well, this implies that they might likewise want to develop the relationship.

This works so reliably that it's feasible to make outright outsiders click with one another by delicately provoking them to uncover personal data to one another - like their most profound privileged insights or fears. In one review, understudies who'd never met before were told to talk with one another, representing a progression of examining and progressively personal inquiries.

The outcome?

A significant number of the members clicked as a result of the experience and created companionships with one another that endured consistently.

This component wherein one individual's receptiveness and weakness drive someone else to open up is unequivocally the very methodology that the prisoner arbitrator utilizes.

To acquire an impact on the strained, temperamental prisoner taker, the arbitrator attempts to interface with him. He trusts that the very perfect second will share a tough spot from his existence with the capturer. Furthermore, whenever he's procured the capturer's trust, the two of them snap and it becomes conceivable to de-raise what is happening.

With regards to connecting, spatial closeness likewise has an influence.

For quite a while, coming out on top for a b-ball title appeared to be far off for the Florida Gators. Their possibilities appeared to be far and away more terrible when the very best players left.

In any case, that was the specific second when their karma started to change: four new colleagues played together so well that the Gators dominated 17 back-to-back matches.

How? Those players who'd clicked so well on the court additionally turned out to be flatmates.

Without a doubt, the nearer you genuinely are to an individual, the more noteworthy the opportunity that you'll become companions.

Think about this review: Trainees in a police foundation were relegated seats in sequential request. Afterward, when they were approached to name those companions whom they'd framed cozy associations with, the vast majority of recruits named the individual sitting close to them.

As this shows, simply being genuinely close to someone else is a preferable indicator of social holding over different standards like age or shared interests.

Be that as it may, why would that be? Essentially, being close to somebody works with unconstrained correspondence and that correspondence prompts holding.

The closer you are to somebody, the more open doors there are for you to start up a discussion. Furthermore, with each discussion you have, you learn something about one another. Moreover, each time you talk, your points of view adjust nearer and nearer.

The impact of closeness on connecting can likewise be found in the peculiarity in which many individuals see recognizable individuals as more appealing.

In one examination, four similarly appealing ladies were told to go to a brain research course in an enormous auditorium. Meanwhile, they were approached to stay away from all collaborations with their kindred understudies.

One lady was to go to each meeting and the others were to go to ten, five or not a solitary one of them.

At the point when different understudies were approached to rate the ladies' engaging quality, not very many of them reviewed in any event, seeing the ladies, however, the greater part of those understudies favored the ladies who'd gone to most of the classes.

Struggle can prompt further, stronger bonds.

The Japanese word kintsugi, or "brilliant fix," alludes to the specialty of retouching broken earthenware. A combination of polish and powdered gold, silver, or platinum is utilized as the paste, making sparkling lines that feature the breaks. In being fixed, the messed up object turns out to be ostensibly more gorgeous.

A more extensive way of thinking is implanted in this methodology: harmed objects have a set of experiences that ought to be commended as opposed to concealed. Similar turns out as expected for connections that have encountered "breaks." By getting the pieces and fixing them with care, your subsequent connections will be more grounded than at any time in recent memory.

The key message is this: Contention can prompt further, stronger bonds.

Interesting issues can be raised and settled with four critical thinking stages that consolidate the conduct input model. Managing struggle beneficially is the fifth sign of an extraordinary relationship, so how about we make a plunge?

In the first place, get the other individual to genuinely take the issue. This could mean letting your accomplice know what her way of behaving is meaning for you, or referencing that her activities aren't by recently talked about objectives. You could likewise find out if you're successfully influencing her way of behaving; recognizing your job can help other people assume a sense of ownership with theirs.

Second, inspire her to share completely what's the deal with her. You can never expect you can read the other individual's mind - issues are much of the time complex and multifaceted, and perhaps the issue you're worried about isn't exactly the fundamental or generally argumentative one.

The third stage is showing up at a commonly fulfilling arrangement. Oppose the compulsion to make do with the base just to end a troublesome discussion; truly ensure the two individuals are fulfilled. Know that this could take some time and include more than one discussion.

At long last, figure out what fix work should be finished. Has the cycle brought about to put you in a terrible mood or made statements you lament? Begin with a straightforward however genuine "Please accept my apologies." By setting aside your pride and expressing a desire for peace, you can mitigate metaphorical injuries and energize complementary weakness. There's a proviso: you need to mean it! Past a conciliatory sentiment, telling your accomplice or partner the amount you esteem her and the relationship can likewise go quite far - as can checking in with her the following day.

You most likely will not promptly feel alright with struggle; as we probably are aware, well-established propensities are difficult to overhaul. Be that as it may, on the off chance that you center around becoming equipped with conflict, the rest will follow. New conduct pathways will result from training and industriousness, so continue - and honor your interaction. Eventually, "the main misstep isn't gaining from your slip-ups."

Value the power and scope of feelings.

Own your feelings or they will possess you. We've all heard the aphorism, that continuing in this day and age can be troublesome. Feelings are much of the time undermined in the working environment and schools, where the accentuation is on reason and rationale.

Subsequently, when we in all actuality do communicate our sentiments, we will more often than not make light of their force. Furthermore, since we're so used to desensitizing ourselves, we frequently don't perceive what we're genuinely feeling - whether fortunate or unfortunate. As Brené Earthy colored notes, "When we numb indignation, bitterness, and dread, we additionally numb appreciation, love, and satisfaction."

Here is the key message: Appreciate the power and scope of feelings.

Disregarding our feelings isn't sound — and when we attempt to cover our sentiments, we will more often than not spill them at any rate. Our tone could turn out to be sharp, or we'll unwittingly articulate a declaration of disdain, which will most likely increment brokenness in a relationship.

Additionally, not managing complaints can prompt acceleration. The creators characterize "squeezes" as seemingly insignificant details that irritate us - for instance, when somebody makes a joke without regard to us. We might protest, or perhaps we'll just allow it to go unaddressed. Notwithstanding, on the off chance that a squeeze gets under our skin and isn't managed, it'll putrefy and develop into an issue that is difficult to disregard, or what the creators call a "crunch." This is when close-to-home blasts occur.

Humor can be utilized to raise, and stop squeezes before they explode, however it can likewise blow up as a result of its questionable nature. The main sure way to goal is to figure out our requirements and express them without holding back. The capacity to be straightforward with one another is, as a matter of fact, the fourth sign of an extraordinary relationship.

Our feelings signal what means quite a bit to us. Furthermore, the more feelings we feel, the almost certain it is that there's something more profound going on. Be that as it may, to take advantage of their abundance of understanding, we first need to develop mindfulness. Here, substantial reactions like an adjustment of heartbeat, vacillating in our stomachs, snugness in our throats, or clammy palms can offer significant hints.

One more method for encouraging mindfulness is to stop amidst a contention - rather than falling back on the rationale, take a stab at asking yourself, What am I, or they, truly feeling? Know that outrage is a particularly troublesome feeling to interpret. That is because it's an optional inclination, frequently used to conceal more weak sentiments like dismissal or jealousy.

It's essential to take note of that, in some random circumstances, we have numerous options for how to answer. Having confidence in our capacity to act on the planet is what social researchers allude to as "having the office." It's never that we can't do or say something; it's that we decide not to. Of the time, saying nothing is the best game plan - however, that is likewise a decision.

In a projecting meeting, up to 100 entertainers read similar lines. The vast majority of them are exceptionally enthusiastic, and many are capable, yet soon enough every one of the tryouts begins to mix.

Then, at that point, one entertainer shows up and the environment changes. Out of nowhere, for reasons unknown, the lines sound perfect.

Whether it's to win a tryout or sparkle as a performer, a noteworthy presentation is conceivable just when an individual is completely submerged in the job that needs to be done. Or on the other hand, the expressions of clinicians researching extraordinary execution, in a "stream express": a condition of complete yet easy fixation which can be reached exclusively by specialists.

Moreover, spellbinding a group of people implies being completely drawn in with your presentation as well as with the actual onlookers. On the off chance that an entertainer isn't receptive to the state of mind of a group of people, then, at that point, regardless of how splendid the presentation, connecting becomes unimaginable.

Simply consider an extraordinary professional comic whose act for the most part "kills." On the off chance that on one night the observers are disturbed, he would do well to peruse and answer their prompts or he won't make them chuckle.

On the off chance that an entertainer is both in a stream state and completely drawn in with the crowd, then, at that point, his verve will spread through the crowd like an infection. This peculiarity is an impact of a "reflecting" process, which is intervened by reflecting neurons in the cerebrum.

For instance, when you notice an individual who's in extraordinary aggravation, this will enact specific cells in the district of your cerebrum related to torment. The outcome is that you'll in all probability feel a less than overwhelming torment, even though you're not entirely stung.

A similar sort of neurological disease happens when an entertainer is in a stream state. Like that entertainer, the crowd will before long wind up profoundly submerged in the presentation.

We're more ready to interface with individuals who are like us.

We'd all prefer to trust that we're magnanimous individuals, ready to give to any advantageous objective.

Be that as it may, think about this investigation: Numerous ladies are drawn nearer by somebody raising assets for a foundation and answer by giving a specific sum. Then, at that point, the asset raiser wears an ID bearing a similar name as the ladies she draws near. What occurs? The gifts were twofold.

This is because we will more often than not favor individuals like ourselves. Without a doubt, we frequently for the most part rate such individuals as more appealing, and, in one examination, understudies who were persuaded to think that a specific outsider shared their perspective found that individual exceptionally appealing.

This comparability predisposition additionally stretches out to other positive ascribes. In the past model, the understudies apparent the more interesting and appealing as well as clever, proficient, and moral.

Such similitudes can lead us to put resources into those connections in light of them. In one examination, members who were approached by an understudy to evaluate a paper she'd composed were two times as liable to consent to make it happen on the off chance that they accepted that the understudy had a similar birthday.

So what's behind this peculiarity?

We will generally consider and treat the people who share characteristics with us as individuals from our "in-bunch" - or, at the end of the day, as family. That is, we generally partner the presence of comparative characteristics with familial relations. Since relatives are generally the individuals who care about us the most and because we share numerous qualities with our families - like wavy hair, spots, and nearsightedness - those individuals who share characteristics practically speaking with us have a greatly improved potential for success of turning into our dear companions.

So to become friends with somebody, you ought to zero in on your similitudes or shared attributes and qualities. The equivalent goes for nailing a prospective employee meeting: attempt to unpretentiously raise an interest you share for all intents and purposes with the questioner. Furthermore, obviously, on the off chance that you believe individuals should give cash, let them know you have a similar name!

Having a place we belong and conquering difficulty together can us in connecting .

In their perspiration hold-up functions, Local Americans cluster in a minuscule cottage and persevere through the mind-boggling heat together.

It doesn't take long for them to interface; they start by sharing accounts of their lives and soon a significant number of them become close to home and cry.

Be that as it may, for what reason does this movement provoke such extraordinary and personal association?

One explanation is that individuals are united by shared affliction. Dealing with a shared adversary can draw out a feeling of brotherhood - as, for instance when partners consolidate in their abhorrence of a perverted chief.

Moreover, by persevering and getting through difficulties together individuals can share an extraordinary close-to-home involvement with which they make themselves defenseless by disregarding being considerate or keeping up with the profound obstructions, similar to the public personas they use to safeguard themselves in regular day-to-day existence.

The such closeness between individuals is the texture of the local area and on the off chance that a local area is characterized, it's bound to click. This is because the clear-cut jobs and boundaries of those networks make such moment associations between individuals conceivable.

For example, in a club or clan, individuals can let down their protections and make themselves defenseless and in this manner expect that any mysteries they've shared are protected inside the gathering. This goes some way toward making sense of the shock that happens when a part uncovers restricted intel to the overall population - whether it's by exposing a previously closeted gay individual or spilling to the sensationalist newspapers a compromising photo from a selective confidential party.

Additionally, in the gatherings of a characterized local area like a club or faction, individuals are compelled or urged to be genuinely near one another consistently. What's more, at long last, being important for a similar gathering produces a feeling of comparability and having a place. Both of these variables are essential to the chance of making moment associations - to connecting.

Weakness emerges from strength, not shortcomings.

The second sign of an extraordinary relationship is that both of you will be defenseless. Presently, there's subtlety in the idea of weakness. Essentially uncovering individual things about yourself isn't exactly defenseless on the off chance that you know how others will respond - there's no gamble included. Sharing when you're uncertain about the response to your revelation, be that as it may, brings others closer.

The key message is this: Weakness emerges from strength, not shortcomings.

This carries us to the third, the firmly related sign of an extraordinary relationship, which is believing that self-revelations will not be utilized against you. Individuals frequently stress that revelation, particularly concerning apparent "surrenders," will cause them to appear to be powerless.

Pioneers, for instance, may think sharing anything that shakes their godlike outside will hurt their height. Be that as it may, as a general rule, nothing could be farther from reality. It takes determination to self-uncover. Your companions will perceive, and respect, this - and utilize your revelation as a model for their straightforwardness.

While weakness welcomes closeness, quietness does the inverse. The less we uncover, the more others will reach determinations to get a handle on what they see. By being hesitant with self-revelation, we fail to keep a grip on how others see us. What's more, when individuals see us a specific way, we frequently wind up putting on a good show, making a negative criticism circle of misleading fronts. The expense of this is disengagement - concerning both our connections and our healthy identity.

In your way of behaving, you might perceive the dangerous slant of made-up anecdotes about someone else in the long run as becoming reductive marks. To counter it, take a stab at making an alternate story about that individual. This could acquaint sufficient vulnerability to drive you back to the drawing board: credulous interest and a receptive outlook.

Discussing interest, while managing self-divulgences, you'll have to step into a scarcely discernible difference between being interested and being meddlesome. Nobody needs to feel like an example under a magnifying instrument. To avoid this expected entanglement, you want to meet individuals where they are. Be that as it may, how? All things considered, by uncovering first, you're bound to construct trust, gain acknowledgment, and get response weakness consequently.

In the meantime, you can assist with building conditions in which others feel more open to acting naturally. Avoid compassion and exhortation, which are seldom valuable; rarely would individuals need to be felt sorry for or determined what to do. All things considered, ways of behaving like listening effectively, suspending judgment, utilizing inquiries without a right or wrong answer, tuning in for feelings, communicating compassion, and showing acknowledgment will energize others' full articulation.

Certain individuals have characteristics that make them more inclined to click with others.

For what reason are certain individuals generally at the focal point of a gathering? How can it be that when these individuals require a brief time frame trip, they get back with a crowd of new companions? You could sensibly think about what makes them so appealing. Without a doubt, it's not only their looks. Isn't that so?

It's not. Such individuals are essentially better receptive to anything that social circumstance they wind up in, in two explicit ways:

In the first place, they're more disposed to see meaningful gestures and act fittingly on them. Since such is not entirely set in stone to be wonderful to other people and to act fittingly in friendly circumstances, they've fostered an uplifted responsiveness toward the states of mind of others and a circumstance's social setting.

For instance, on the off chance that such an individual is partaking in a personal supper in a heartfelt eatery, she will effectively accurately distinguish the climate - the circumstance's social setting - and adjust her voice level to fit with the climate.

Such individuals are additionally ready to promptly see if, in the discussion, their sidekick becomes exhausted - and they'll change the subject immediately.

The second way that these individuals are more delicate to social settings is that they're more mindful of their self-show and more proficient at changing it to the requirements of others. As such individuals are anxious to please, they are leaned to screen their non-verbal communication and close-to-home correspondence with the goal that they can change it at whatever point fundamentally.

So whether their sidekick is in the state of mind to invest energy with a gregarious individual or a quiet and calm one, an unapproachable individual or a mindful and mindful companion, the snap-inclined individual will regulate their way of behaving to supplement the other's way of behaving and to give them what they need.

As friendly chameleons, such individuals can bargain proficiently with a different exhibit of characters, causing everybody to feel quiet and could intercede between contradictory individuals.

The critical message in this book:

However, it feels otherworldly when we are in a split-second interface with a person or thing, there are unmistakable variables that are the premise of such "click" minutes - including closeness, receptiveness, and shared characteristics. At the point when we click with somebody, this can loan an extraordinary quality to the relationship that will describe it for the length. Additionally, groups that snap are significantly more useful than groups that don't.

Significant exhortation:

Figure out something worth agreeing on.

At the point when you need to become friends with somebody, center around the similitudes you share. Regularly, he or she'll find you significantly more appealing when they figure out that you both offer unmistakable characteristics.